Jonathan Maitland

Dead Sheep

Geoffrey, Elspeth and the death of Margaret Thatcher

Salamander Street

PLAYS

First published in 2020 by Salamander Street Ltd.
(info@salamanderstreet.com.)

Dead Sheep © Jonathan Maitland, 2020

ISBN: 9781913630782

Printed and bound in Great Britain

10 9 8 7 6 5 4 3 2 1

Dramatis Personae
(Cast of 6)

GEOFFREY HOWE

ELSPETH HOWE

MARGARET THATCHER

MINISTER 1
(CHARLES POWELL, ALAN CLARK,
BERNARD INGHAM, JOHN REDWOOD,
NEIL KINNOCK, BILL CASH.)

MINISTER 2
(STEPHEN WALL, BRIAN WALDEN, HACK.)

MINISTER 3
(IAN GOW, DENNIS THATCHER,
NIGEL LAWSON, SPEAKER.)

Act 1

SCENE 1

1989. **GEOFFREY** *mid-stage, thoughtful, contemplative. Sfx: chatter, clinking glasses.* **ELSPETH**, **MARGARET** *and the* **MINISTERS** *enter.* **GEOFFREY** *taps his glass with a spoon.*

GEOFFREY: Ah, if I may everybody? Thank you. *(Clears throat, readies himself.)*

MINISTER 2: *(Quietly, to audience.)* Prepare to be bored rigid!

GEOFFREY: Ten years ago today, Margaret Thatcher became our first woman Prime Minister. It has been a dizzying time. It began on May the 4th 1979 with our Economy on the brink. Inflation 20 per cent, unemployment two million. Dark days.

MINISTER 1 *yawns hugely, stifles it.*

But salvation came via M3.

The money supply not the motorway.

Polite, dutiful laughter.

Which like its namesake, began to flow less than freely. Thus taming inflation. The numbers are instructive. Margaret has outlasted four Japanese Prime Ministers, eleven Italian governments and forty-seven cabinet colleagues.

Genuine titters.

History will recognise her as a leader who assailed the conventional wisdom, changed the political map and put her country back on its feet again.

Silence. **ELSPETH** *leads light round of applause.*

IAN: *(Effusive.)* Here here! And may I just add if I may?
(**GEOFFREY** *nods.*) That when Geoffrey and I were young men starting out on life in politics with a deep love of school, party and country binding us together, how many times would we stay up late quaffing Drambuie by the bucket, talking about how we would keep Britain great? Geoffrey! How many times would we do that?

GEOFFREY: Er – many times. Many times!

IAN: Exactly. Then along comes this marvellous woman who is literally the answer to our prayers. Because she has done as much as anyone in our history to keep Britain Great. So God bless Margaret Thatcher and all who sail in her.

Chorus of "for she's a jolly good fellow" halts mid-verse. **ELSPETH**, **GEOFFREY** *and* **MARGARET** *freeze.*

MINISTER 1: *(To audience.)* That, was Ian Gow.

MINISTER 2: *(To audience.)* Geoffrey's oldest pal, but also, loyal Thatcherite.

IAN GOW: Loyal? Bloody smitten.

MINISTER 1: Quite. *(To* **MINISTER TWO**.*)* So who are we?

MINISTER 2: Well we, that is the three of us, could be anyone in the next minutes, hours and years.

GOW/MINISTER 3: Yes. *(To audience.)* But this is politics, so we will keep you the electorate, informed.

MARGARET, **GEOFFREY** and **ELSPETH** *unfreeze.*

MINISTER 2: Er Ian. *(Points to* **MARGARET**. **IAN** *goes to her, fawns.)* Poor Geoffrey. Couldn't they have got someone else to do the speech?

MINISTER 1: Like who?

MINISTER 2: I dunno? President Reagan?

MINISTER 1: I'm not sure he's classy enough.

MINISTER 2: *(To audience.)* And American Presidents should always be classy.

MINISTER 1: I suppose it had to be Geoffrey.

MINISTER 2: He's no Martin Luther King though, is he?

MINISTER 1: He does suck the life out of the text rather. Imagine him doing "I have a dream". He'd make it sound like the phone book. *(Imitates* **GEOFFREY**.*)* "I have a dream, that one day, people won't nod off when I speak."

MINISTER 2: I have a dream that one day he'll say what he really thinks.

MINISTER 1: What, "she can't stand me but she can't get rid of me so there"? Ha. Hasn't got the balls.

MINISTER 2: Unlike you know who.

MINISTER 1: Mmm.*(Looks at* **MARGARET**.*)* Isn't she wonderful?

MINISTER 2: No not her you idiot. His wife. Elspeth.

MINISTER 1: Oh Lord. Boadicea Mark Two.

MINISTER 2: Have you heard the story about their wedding?

MINISTER 1: What, the Howes'? Go on.

MINISTER 2: Apparently Elspeth had her fingers crossed during the ceremony because she was appalled at having to say the words "Love, honour and obey". Tried to edit them out but the vicar refused.

MINISTER 1: Why was she appalled?

MINISTER 2: You don't 'obey' someone who's your equal. Feminist.

MINISTER 1: Oh God. Actually Margaret believes in equal opportunities.

MINISTER 2: Really?

MINISTER 1: Yes. She believes everyone should have the opportunity to be insulted by her, equally.

GEOFFREY *starts the introductions.*

Oop. It's meet the wives time.

MINISTER 1: Watch out for the handshake manoeuvre.

MINISTER 2: What?

MINISTER 1: She can't stand talking to them, so when she shakes their hands she just yanks them out the way. Brilliant.

MARGARET and ELSPETH shake hands.

MARGARET tries to yank her out the way, ELSPETH stands firm. This standing dance lasts several seconds.

MINISTER 2: Irresistible force meets immoveable object.

GEOFFREY: *(To MARGARET.)* No need to introduce –

MARGARET: Hello dear –

ELSPETH: Good evening Prime Minister, congratulations.

MARGARET: Thank you. Have you had a good evening?

ELSPETH: Yes thank you. Good to be here. We don't often get invited. As you know.

MARGARET: We always like to include the wives. When we can. And how is your – Commission?

ELSPETH: Equal Opportunities or Broadcasting Standards?

MARGARET: Both.

ELSPETH: Oh the fight goes on. Especially on the discrimination front. There's a lot of it about you know. Particularly against women. Funnily enough. Prime Minister.

MARGARET: Of course some of us didn't need that kind of thing to get on you know. We did it ourselves.

ELSPETH: Not every woman is like you Prime Minister.

MARGARET: Do you know I always think the best thing a woman can do is stay home, look after the house and raise a family.

ELSPETH: Really?

MARGARET: I did my fair share dear. And I have twins: they need less looking after.

ELSPETH: Really? I must tell that to my twins.

MARGARET, ELSPETH *exit in opposite directions.*

MINISTER 1: Wow. Out of the lion's den and barely a scratch.

MINISTER 2: Yes. But what about the rumblings?

MINISTER 1: What about them?

MINISTER 2: They're getting louder…

MINISTER 1: You need more than rumblings to remove Margaret. Anyway who's going to start the earthquake? Captain Mainwaring over there? He's not the earthquake type.

MINISTER 2: What do they do at home? The Thatchers and the Howes?

MINISTER 1: As my father used to say. No one knows what goes on between a man and a woman. Only God. And sometimes, not even him.

The **MINISTERS** *exit.*

SCENE 2

That night. The bedrooms of the **HOWES** *and the* **THATCHERS**.

ELSPETH: What's wrong?

GEOFFREY: *(Off stage.)* Nothing.

ELSPETH: Come on. What is it?

GEOFFREY: The trouser press isn't working.

ELSPETH: And? Come on.

    GEOFFREY *enters, in dressing gown and short socks with gaiters.*

GEOFFREY: What did you think of my speech?

ELSPETH: I knew it was that. It was good. I liked the joke about the money supply.

GEOFFREY: And the truth?

ELSPETH: It was good. In the circumstances.

GEOFFREY: Go on.

ELSPETH: Hard to be heartfelt when your heart's not in it.

GEOFFREY: I know. I felt like a fraud.

ELSPETH: You meant some of it.

GEOFFREY: Which makes me not much better than a double glazing salesman.

ELSPETH: But a good politician.

GEOFFREY: The dice is somewhat loaded. Ian's specialist subject is Margaret Thatcher, a woman he loves. Mine, is the hard ECU. Not quite as audience friendly.

ELSPETH: That's rather good. You see, you are capable of it.

GEOFFREY: 'Capable'? I don't like capable. It suggests potential unfulfilled.

ELSPETH: Your curriculum vitae doesn't look unfulfilled to me. Chancellor and Foreign Secretary.

GEOFFREY: Exactly. There are three great offices of state. I, have achieved only two.

MARGARET *working.* **DENIS** *off-stage, in toilet.*

MARGARET: Denis?

DENIS: Yes love?

Toilet flushes. **MARGARET** *winces.*

MARGARET: I think she's behind it you know.

DENIS: Behind what? Who?

MARGARET: The plotting. They're plotting against me. Him. And her.

DENIS: That's what politicians do isn't it? You know, every soldier has a Field Marshall's baton in his knapsack and all that.

MARGARET: It's the way they go on, Nigel and the others, when they've been to Chevening, about what a wonderful time they've had. She's setting him up. Tedious, boring little Geoffrey is being trained by his wife to take my place.

DENIS: You think so love? Doesn't seem like the plotting type. Plodding, more like.

MARGARET: But why invite Ian and Nigel down there if they're not hatching something?

DENIS: Because they're friends?

Focus on **GEOFFREY** *and* **ELSPETH**.

ELSPETH: Who've we invited this weekend again?

GEOFFREY: The Gows and possibly the Lawsons.

ELSPETH: Super. If Nigel comes we'll need extra canapés. Lots. We can use the mint and asparagus from the herb garden. Joy!

GEOFFREY: We could play that game in the Maze.

ELSPETH: Oh yes great fun. I'm giving a speech in Scotland Friday, staying overnight, might be a bit late. You'll manage?

GEOFFREY: I am the Foreign Secretary. I think I will.

Back on **MARGARET/DENIS**.

DENIS: That Champagne was camel's piss love. Her Majesty's Government can't serve that to its cabinet. You should have a word. So what was Howe's Mrs on about?

MARGARET: Equal rights. For women.

DENIS: Bloody hell. You know what her problem is don't you? Her real problem?

MARGARET: No?

DENIS: Jealous. She's running some poxy pinko thing for lesbos and you're PM.

Back on **ELSPETH/GEOFFREY**.

GEOFFREY: How did you get on with the Prime Minister?

11

ELSPETH: How do you think?

GEOFFREY: Did she ask you to join the cabinet?

ELSPETH: I will let her have my decision presently.

GEOFFREY: Did you agree on anything?

ELSPETH: Yes. We agreed to disagree. On everything. It's the eyes. Have you looked in them?

GEOFFREY: One tries not to these days.

ELSPETH: Like an executioner's. How do you do it?

GEOFFREY: Loyalty.

Back on **MARGARET/DENIS**.

MARGARET: He has no loyalty that man. And he is quite, quite wrong about Europe.

DENIS: I know. Where are my earplugs?

MARGARET: I asked for them to be washed.

DENIS: Damn.

MARGARET: Do you want me to look for them?

DENIS: It's all right love. I'll improvise.

Good night.

MARGARET: *(Puts pen down.)* Denis?

DENIS: Yes love?

MARGARET: Is there anything you want me to, do for you?

DENIS: 'S alright love.

MARGARET: Are you sure?

DENIS: I think so.

MARGARET: *(Beat.)* Are you quite sure?

DENIS: Erm – yes. I am.

MARGARET: Good. *(Carries on working.)*

ELSPETH: But *why* are you so loyal to her?

GEOFFREY: *(Sighs.)* Do we have to? Goodnight.

ELSPETH exits. **DENIS** *snores.* **MARGARET** *exits.*

SCENE 3

1981. Cabinet. **GEOFFREY** *next to* **MARGARET**. **MINISTERS** *enter.*

MINISTER 1: Do you remember 1981?

MINISTER 2: Oh yes. '81. The country was in a hell of a state.

MINISTER 3: The economy was in tatters.

MINISTER 2: There was rioting in the streets.

MINISTER 1: And Margaret's ratings were in the toilet.

MINISTER 3: They wanted her out.

MINISTER 1: We all did.

MINISTER 3: Female Prime Minister. Never works.

MINISTER 2: It all hung on Geoffrey's budget.

MINISTER 1: The funny thing is, in the midst of all this shit, they were actually getting on rather well.

MINISTER 3: Who, Margaret and Geoffrey?

MINISTER 2: Yes. Very well in fact.

They sit at the cabinet table.

MARGARET: Good morning gentlemen.

MINISTERS: Good morning Prime Minister.

MARGARET: Now, the Budget. It will contain stiff medicine but I have discussed this with Geoffrey. We cannot let things go on as they are.

MINISTER 1: So correct me if I'm wrong, Prime Minister, but if I understand the rather sketchy outline we are going to be putting taxes UP, in effect?

MARGARET: We would not contradict you on that no.

MINISTER 3: But Prime Minister we were not elected to put taxes up.

MINISTER 2: Exactly! How's it going to look when our budget clobbers families in difficulty by putting income tax up?

MINISTER 3: It's a recession for goodness sake. Prime Minister I fear we are making a serious mistake.

MARGARET: If I may explain. The tax rises are –

GEOFFREY: Prime Minister, if I may. While it is indeed the case that the tax burden as a whole will go up, what I will announce is not an income tax increment as such, which would be unpopular, but rather a freeze in income tax allowances which, when one takes inflation into account, is likely to yield two billion pounds. May I suggest gentlemen you wait for the detail of the budget before criticising its perceived consequences?

MINISTER 1: Useful to have a man who knows what's going on under the bonnet, eh?

Laughter. **MARGARET** *eyeballs him.*

(Squirming.) That was a joke.

MINISTER 2: Um, Prime Minister?

MARGARET: Yes?

MINISTER 2: What about the letter in *The Times*? Signed by no fewer than 364 economists, every single one of whom thinks Geoffrey's doing the wrong thing.

MARGARET *looks at* **GEOFFREY**.

GEOFFREY: I am reminded of the definition of an economist. An economist, is a man who knows 364 ways of making love... but doesn't know any women.

Laughter.

MARGARET: Very good! That will be all gentlemen.

MINISTERS *exit,* **GEOFFREY** *starts to.*

Ah Geoffrey? *(Beat.)* Thank you.

GEOFFREY: Not at all. I am with you Margaret, as you know. But we must hold firm. It's not easy though, being believers in a cabinet full of those who don't.

MARGARET: "Holding firm", I can do. What I find difficult …

GEOFFREY: Yes?

MARGARET: Just then, I wasn't quite able to – . I just wanted to thank you for your interjections. I am most grateful.

GEOFFREY: *(Beat.)* Are you all right Margaret?

MARGARET: Yes.

GEOFFREY: Margaret it is important we are honest with each other. *(Carefully.)* And you must know, because I certainly do, that to admit weakness is a strength. We are talking as friends now, confidantes –?

MARGARET: Yes of course.

GEOFFREY: Would that be, broadly, your zone of thinking?

MARGARET: *(Beat.)* Yes Geoffrey it would broadly be that. We are talking in confidence now?

GEOFFREY: We are.

MARGARET: When you are Prime Minister you are supposed to know everything. How to cure inflation, who the President of Mexico is, what coal mines are the most productive, everything. You are simply not allowed, to not know everything. And you can't of course. But you can't admit that: you can't say "I'm sorry, I don't know the answer", because you are Prime Minister. Do you understand?

GEOFFREY: Oh yes. I'm Chancellor of the Exchequer and even I find some financial concepts hard to grasp.

MARGARET: Really? Such as?

GEOFFREY: The non-linear dynamics of economic yield curves.

MARGARET: The what?

GEOFFREY: The non-linear dynamics of economic yield curves.

MARGARET: What are they?

GEOFFREY: Exactly.

MARGARET: Oh.

GEOFFREY: It's not knowledge that makes a leader, it's judgment. Indeed sometimes, one can know too much. So may I suggest you worry less, and where appropriate, trust a little more.

MARGARET: Thank you Geoffrey. And can I trust you?

GEOFFREY: Of course!

MARGARET: Thank you Geoffrey.

GEOFFREY: Thank you Margaret.

  MINISTERS *enter.*

MINISTER 3: That was nice.

MINISTER 1: So when did it all go wrong?

  Or start to?

MINISTER 2: Do you know, I think it was when she got good, at winning elections.

SCENE 4

The 1983 conservative conference. **MARGARET** *standing,* **GEOFFREY** *seated next to* **MINISTERS**.

MARGARET: We meet in the aftermath of a great victory. I think we can say the result was not exactly a photo-finish. *(Laughter, applause.)* We were elected to tackle problems others had shirked. The pessimists said it could not be done. They under-estimated three things: This Government, the British people, and you, Geoffrey.

Rapturous applause, **GEOFFREY**, *surprised, acknowledges it*

MINISTER 1: So far, so good!

MINISTER 2: Yes but then the air began to seep out of the balloon somewhat. Remember?

MINISTER 1: Oh yes.

Reception. **ELSPETH** *enters.*

GEOFFREY: Thank you for your kind words Prime Minister.

MARGARET: Geoffrey we could not have done it without you. *(To* **ELSPETH***.)* Hello dear. You must be very proud of him. He has done wonderfully.

ELSPETH: I've always been proud of him.

MARGARET: I do admire him. He may speak in that very low key way of his, but he gets things done. He brings me solutions without upsetting people. Don't you Geoffrey?

GEOFFREY: If you say so.

MARGARET: But there is still a great deal more to do. Isn't there Geoffrey?

GEOFFREY: If you say so.

MARGARET: Geoffrey you do keep saying that but yes, we will not rest, we will not rest until socialism is routed. That is our aim.

ELSPETH: Routed?

MARGARET: *(Looks quizzical.)* Yes dear?

ELSPETH: Routed?

MARGARET: Yes. Routed!

ELSPETH: How – intriguing. Sorry.

MARGARET: Did you not hear my speech?

ELSPETH: Yes. I just –

MARGARET *ignores her, prepares for small talk with* **MINISTER 1**.

– thought it a rather interesting word to use.

MARGARET: Sorry dear what was that?

ELSPETH: Rout. Interesting word.

MARGARET: What word would you use?

ELSPETH: Reformed? Adapted?

MARGARET: Oh dear. You do have a lot to learn. *(To* **MINISTERS.***)* What would, she, have us do to the enemy? Cuddle up to them?

ELSPETH: Well I'm not sure I'd call them the enemy in the first place. And if I had to live with them afterwards I might not want to rout them either. Prime Minister.

MARGARET: I did not win two elections and a war by being nice to people.

> **MARGARET** *turns back on* **ELSPETH** *and walks away.*

ELSPETH: Who knows what you'd achieve if you were?

> **MARGARET** *turns round.*

MARGARET: I beg your pardon?

ELSPETH: I said who knows what you might achieve if you were nicer to people.

MARGARET: Which people did you have in mind?

ELSPETH: All right then. The homeless?

GEOFFREY: *(Trying to interrupt.)* Elspeth –

ELSPETH: *(Cutting across him.)* There are thousands sleeping rough, especially in London, in desperate need of help. Could be a vote winner. Quite apart from being the right thing to do.

MARGARET: I do know that dear and we are doing all we can but I don't think now is the time or place.

ELSPETH: Well you did ask me Prime Minister.

MARGARET: It was rather a rhetorical question dear. You do know what that means?

ELSPETH: I'm not sure there is, such a thing as 'rather a rhetorical question'. It either is, or it isn't. And when is the right time by the way?

MARGARET: What?

ELSPETH: When is the right time to bring up homelessness?

MARGARET: Well as your husband will appreciate, not now. Not here, right now. *(Beat.)* Am I right, Geoffrey?

MARGARET and ELSPETH turn to look at a mortified GEOFFREY.

GEOFFREY: I. Think. That. Healthy debate of any kind is to be encouraged. *(Beat.)* As is the serving of more celebratory drinks. *(Beat.)* Waiter!

ELSPETH and MARGARET exit in opposite directions.

MINISTER 3: Yes that was definitely the start of it.

MINISTER 2: Oh dear. She did owe him though. She couldn't have done it without him.

MINISTER 1: True. But she did pay the debt. She made him Foreign Secretary remember!

MINISTER 2: I know. Talking of which, let's fast forward to 1989 again. Back where our story began.

SCENE 5

1989. A cabinet meeting.

MINISTER 1: Yes and by this time, things had gone well and truly tits up between them.

GEOFFREY and MARGARET at opposite ends of the stage.

MINISTER 3: Yes a certain 'distance' does seem to have developed.

MINISTER 1: I prefer "chasm".

MINISTER 3: Why? What was it all about?

MINISTER 1: Europe. Funny that.

The **MINISTERS** *sit down.*

MARGARET: Now Geoffrey after your not very helpful comments in the papers please summarise, briefly if you will, *(***MINISTERS** *snigger, exchange looks.)* your recent communications with Monsieur Delors.

GEOFFREY: Thank you Prime Minister. I think I speak not just for myself when I say –

MARGARET: Geoffrey please speak up. We can't hear you.

GEOFFREY: Ahem. *(Louder now.)* Yes. I think I speak not just for myself when I say –

MARGARET: Geoffrey you are not speaking very loudly for yourself. Turn it up!

GEOFFREY: *(Louder still.)* Right. I speak not just for myself when I say that quite apart from this issue –

MARGARET: Come on Geoffrey, get on with it!

GEOFFREY: There is the equally significant issue of monetary union, currently being discussed by the committee –

MARGARET: *(Angrily.)* Geoffrey, for goodness' sake please get to the point.

GEOFFREY: The point being that I expect the committee to –

MARGARET: You know what I say about committees Geoffrey.

GEOFFREY: Yes Prime Minister.

MARGARET: Committees. They take minutes…but last for hours! *(Sycophantic laughter, silence.)* Oh do carry on Geoffrey.

GEOFFREY: Yes. The point being I expect the committee to come up with a firm timetable –

MARGARET: Geoffrey is there anything new?

GEOFFREY: If restating the case with renewed urgency can be said to be 'new' Prime Minister, I still feel it is of utmost importance we go to the Madrid Summit with a unified line –

MARGARET: I agree. And don't worry we will of course come up with a line for Madrid we can all agree on. Provided of course, it's acceptable to me. *(Laughter.)* Thank you gentlemen. *(Exiting, to* **GEOFFREY**.*)* Twaddle!

MARGARET *exits.*

SCENE 6

MINISTERS *'create' Chevening.* **GEOFFREY** *fumes.*

MINISTER 3: So where are we now?

MINISTER 2: Aaah this is Chevening. In Kent.

MINISTER 1: Oh yes. A magnificent grace and favour home, the residency of which, is in the gift of the PM.

MINISTER 2: Current occupants? The Foreign Secretary and his wife.

A dog barks.

oh and Summit. The dog.

MINISTER 3: Summit?

MINISTER 2: Yes. Geoffrey wanted something appropriate. *(**MINISTER 2** puzzled.)* Foreign Secretary? Summits?

MINISTER 3: Ha! *(Sarcastic.)* What a card.

MINISTER 2: You should have the name of the previous pooch.

MINISTER 3: What was it?

MINISTER 2: 'Budget'. What a sense of humour eh?

More barking. **MINISTERS** *exit.* **ELSPETH** *enters.*

ELSPETH: Goodness me was it that bad?

GEOFFREY: Yes.

ELSPETH: *(Mock dramatic.)* Don't worry darling. We'll always have Chevening.

GEOFFREY: Yes but only until –

ELSPETH: I know darling. It's a joke.

GEOFFREY: What?

ELSPETH: Haven't you seen Casab– ? Never mind. Have you spoken to Ian?

GEOFFREY: Not yet.

ELSPETH: What are you going to do?

GEOFFREY: Sometimes the best course of action is to do nothing.

ELSPETH: Nothing ever or nothing yet?

GEOFFREY: Well Mr Walden, it is "currently my intention", to do nothing. I'm not Heseltine, I can't prowl the wilderness like a hungry lion. I'm more of a –

ELSPETH: What, bear? A lovely, cuddly bear?

GEOFFREY: Elspeth please. A Foreign Secretary should be many things. But never cuddly.

ELSPETH: I don't know. Could be a good negotiating tactic. How long's it take for a bear's head to get sore?

GEOFFREY: It's been sore for years.

ELSPETH: To be treated that way in Cabinet. Week after week.

GEOFFREY: Yes. If only she could grasp the principle that –

ELSPETH: – you don't demean an officer in front of the troops? I know.

GEOFFREY: It is hard to be the man who designed a great building only for the ribbon cutter to steal his thunder. If that's not immodest.

ELSPETH: No one would accuse you of that.

GEOFFREY: It is – infuriating, in fact.

ELSPETH: You can always walk away Geoffrey. I just worry what this is doing to your self – *(Beat.)* What effect it's having.

GEOFFREY: I think one just has to accept the price of a seat at the table.

ELSPETH: Until one is perhaps in a position to sit at the head of it. And twirl the Field Marshall's baton.

GEOFFREY: Precisely. Though I fear I am one hundred years too late.

ELSPETH: Why?

GEOFFREY: In 1889, the job of Prime Minister required, inter alia, judgment and intellect. In *nineteen* 89, the overriding requirement seems to be – *(Dismissive.)* Being good on television. I am not. All this 'sound bite' nonsense.

ELSPETH: I think you'd make an excellent PM.

GEOFFREY: Thank you.

ELSPETH: Except –

GEOFFREY: What?

ELSPETH: Well who's going to want her battered political husband sitting there?

GEOFFREY: Has it not occurred to you that the politics of the cabinet room are different from those of the bedroom?

ELSPETH: Has it not occurred to you that if someone is bullied they should stand up for themselves?

GEOFFREY: I am perfectly capable of standing up for myself. I am now am I not?

ELSPETH: Exactly. So why not stand up to her?

GEOFFREY: Because she is Prime Minister, because she is ruthless and because she might sack me. One would hope for a little more support and understanding in these circumstances.

ELSPETH: What do you think I've been doing these past thirty-seven years Geoffrey?

SCENE 7

ELSPETH *exits.* **GEOFFREY** *sits at desk, looks at phone.* **MINISTERS 2** *and* **3** *enter.*

MINISTER 3: The problem is, Geoffrey's got an itch, about Europe, which clearly needs a scratch.

MINISTER 2: How do you know?

MINISTER 3: Because he's about to ring me to discuss it. *(Gestures to himself.)* Nigel Lawson. She made me Chancellor, when she made him Foreign Secretary. Quite right too, I was easily the best man for the job.

MINISTER 2: Modest too.

MINISTER 3: Sorry. Nothing to be modest about.

Who are you by the way?

MINISTER 2/STEPHEN: Stephen Wall. Geoffrey's private secretary. Wall by name, wall by nature. Straight, non-porous, bit of a brick.

MINISTER 3/NIGEL: Right.

Following exchanges on phones. **STEPHEN**, *on 1980's mobile, stands between* **GEOFFREY** *and* **NIGEL**, *at desks, on 1970's hang-up phones.* **NIGEL**'s *rings.*

NIGEL: Yes?

GEOFFREY: Nigel it's Geoffrey.

NIGEL: Geoffrey. What are we going to do?

GEOFFREY: What do you think? We fly to Madrid tomorrow night.

NIGEL: We need to meet her. Immediately. Just you, me and her.

GEOFFREY: She won't want that.

NIGEL: I know. But there is no alternative. We have to state our position firmly, before Madrid. So it has to be now.

GEOFFREY: Yes. Just the three of us. I see that. *(Beat.)* Shall I do it?

NIGEL: You're the one going to Madrid.

GEOFFREY: Yes. Right.

GEOFFREY *calls* **STEPHEN**. *We hear children, playing.*

STEPHEN: Stephen Wall?

GEOFFREY: Stephen. We need to meet the Prime Minister. Nigel and I. Before we fly.

STEPHEN: I'll put a request in.

GEOFFREY: Thank you. Where are you by the way? Some sort of parade?

STEPHEN: It's my youngest's sports day.

GEOFFREY: Oh. Nice. Good luck.

> **STEPHEN** *calls* **POWELL.**

VOICE OF POWELL: Hello?

STEPHEN: Charles it's Stephen. The Foreign Secretary and Chancellor want to meet the PM before Madrid. Is it do-able?

VOICE OF POWELL: She won't be keen.

STEPHEN: I know.

VOICE OF POWELL: I'll ask.

STEPHEN: Thanks.

> **STEPHEN** *calls* **GEOFFREY.**
>
> Charles says she won't be keen.
>
> But he'll ask.

GEOFFREY: Thank you.

> **STEPHEN** *looks at phone, answers.*

STEPHEN: Stephen Wall.

VOICE OF POWELL: Hasn't got the time. Sorry.

STEPHEN: Are you sure? Right.

> **STEPHEN** *calls* **GEOFFREY.**
>
> Hasn't got the time. Apparently.

GEOFFREY: Right.

> **GEOFFREY** *calls* **NIGEL.**

GEOFFREY: She won't do it.

NIGEL: Why not?

GEOFFREY: Hasn't got the time. Apparently.

NIGEL: We cannot not meet her. This is a matter of great national importance.

GEOFFREY: I know. I'll call you back.

> **GEOFFREY** *calls* **STEPHEN**.

GEOFFREY: Would you try again? And make it clear we need to see her?

STEPHEN: I'll get back to you.

GEOFFREY: Thank you.

> **STEPHEN** *calls* **POWELL**.

STEPHEN: They need to see her Charles. Could you ask again please?

VOICE OF POWELL: She doesn't want this.

STEPHEN: I know. But Geoffrey and Nigel do.

VOICE OF POWELL: I'll ask. Again.

STEPHEN: Thanks.

> **STEPHEN** *calls* **GEOFFREY**.

He's asking again. Fingers crossed.

GEOFFREY: Thank you.

> **STEPHEN** *looks at his watch. Then phone. Answers it.*

STEPHEN: Stephen Wall?

VOICE OF POWELL: No.

STEPHEN: Look, Charles – okay.

> **STEPHEN** *calls* **GEOFFREY**.

STEPHEN: Still no.

GEOFFREY: I'll call you back.

> **GEOFFREY** *calls* **NIGEL**.

Still no I'm afraid.

NIGEL: Right. Tell her *(Beat.)* we won't take no for an answer.

GEOFFREY: Are you sure?

NIGEL: Aren't you?

GEOFFREY: Yes. I am.

> **GEOFFREY** *calls* **STEPHEN**.

We *(Beat.)* won't take no for an answer.

STEPHEN: Are you sure?

GEOFFREY: Yes.

> **STEPHEN** *calls* **POWELL**.

STEPHEN: They won't take no for an answer. On this occasion.

VOICE OF POWELL: Right.

> **STEPHEN** *clicks off, redials.*

STEPHEN: He's calling me back.

GEOFFREY: When?

STEPHEN: Any second now I expect.

> *Clicks off. Looks at phone. Then clicks on again.*

STEPHEN: Stephen Wall?

VOICE OF POWELL: Seven o'clock tomorrow morning. Her office.

STEPHEN: Good God! Thank you.

VOICE OF POWELL: Good luck.

> **STEPHEN** *calls* **GEOFFREY**.

STEPHEN: Seven o'clock, tomorrow morning, her office.

GEOFFREY: Goodness. Excellent. I think.

> **GEOFFREY** *calls* **NIGEL**.

GEOFFREY: Tomorrow morning, seven o'clock, her office.

NIGEL: Good. See you there.

> **STEPHEN** *exits.*

SCENE 8

Sfx: Big Ben. **MARGARET** *at desk.* **GEOFFREY** *and* **NIGEL** *enter.*

MARGARET: Good morning gentlemen.

GEOFFREY/NIGEL: Morning Prime Minister.

MARGARET: Yes?

GEOFFREY: Indeed Prime Minister. As you know, Nigel and I feel it is of the utmost importance that we move forward on the issue of the European Exchange Rate Mechanism. We believe strongly that we must, absolutely must, announce a firm date for entry at Madrid. Of no later than 1992.

MARGARET: Is that it?

GEOFFREY: I must add Prime Minister, if you feel unable to move forward on these lines then I could – no longer remain a member of the government.

NIGEL: You know Prime Minister if Geoffrey goes I must go too.

MARGARET: Very well gentlemen. I shall reflect on this. Is there anything more?

GEOFFREY/NIGEL: No Prime Minister.

> **MARGARET** *starts working. Silence.*

GEOFFREY: *(Sotto.)* Go go go!

> **GEOFFREY** *and* **NIGEL** *exit.* **MINISTERS 1** *and* **2** *enter.*

MINISTER 1: Breath taking. Don't you think? *(Yorkshire accent.)* And bloody scary.

MINISTER 2: Quite. But why the Yorkshire accent?

MINISTER 1: Bernard Ingham, Margaret's press secretary. You?

MINISTER 2: Stephen Wall still.

MINISTER 1: Right. *(Exits.)*

MINISTER 2: And this is – Madrid actually.

Produces fan. Sfx: spanish guitar.

And Margaret's just made her big speech on Europe. Which I'm delighted to say, was, according to the BBC, quote, 'unexpectedly conciliatory'.

GEOFFREY enters, produces fan.

STEPHEN: That was a surprise!

GEOFFREY: Indeed.

STEPHEN: I think the headline, is "Thatcher softens line on Europe". Great.

GEOFFREY: Yes and did you hear what President Delors said?

STEPHEN: No?

GEOFFREY: Geoffrey mon ami congratulations it seems you have won the intellectual argument with, you-know-who.

STEPHEN: Oh Lord. Hope he didn't tell her that.

GEOFFREY: I doubt it. *(Both exit.)* Yes I must say I'm pleased at the tenor and content of what the Prime Minister had to say.

BERNARD and MARGARET enter.

INGHAM: Very good Prime Minister. Skilful.

MARGARET: Thank you Bernard.

INGHAM: Oldest one in book. 'I can today reaffirm the United Kingdom's intention to join.' Oh we do love an intention. In other words nothing's changed so boogger off.

MARGARET: Quite. Bernard. Did you see Delors' Foreign Secretary? He had a beard.

BERNARD: I know. Containing parts of his breakfast if I'm not mistaken. Oeuf et croissant by the look of it.

MARGARET: You know what I say about men with beards Bernard.

BERNARD: Indeed Prime Minister.

MARGARET: No man with a beard will ever achieve high office in our country. I mean, what are they hiding?

BERNARD: Indeed Prime Minister. Leader of the Opposition perhaps?

MARGARET: Oh no. Not even Labour would elect a man with a beard to lead them.

BERNARD: Yes. Ginger and bald is far as it goes.

MARGARET: Bernard. Did you see the way Delors looked at me? He likes women you know.

BERNARD: Bloody Frenchman. Like a dog on heat.

MARGARET: I rather liked it.

BERNARD: Really?

MARGARET: Yes. I am a woman you know Bernard.

BERNARD: Indeed Prime Minister.

MARGARET: Are you blushing Bernard?

BERNARD: No Prime Minister. I'm from Yorkshire.

MARGARET: Oh and Bernard? I want to see the Chief Whip when we get back. We need to talk about Geoffrey. Time to withdraw our love I think.

BERNARD: Consider it done. By the way nice of you to stick up for that young French lass. You know, the waitress. She was getting a right earful 'til you stepped in.

MARGARET: Thank you Bernard. Always remember the little people.

BERNARD: Indeed!

    BERNARD *and* **MARGARET** *exit.*

SCENE 9

MINISTERS 1 *and* **2** *enter, recreate Chevening.*

MINISTER 2: Chevening is lovely, isn't it?

MINISTER 3: Yes. Not such a lovely atmosphere though.

MINISTER 2: Yes the press very much sense the froideur, between Geoffrey and the PM.

MINISTER 3: Margaret wouldn't like that word.

MINISTER 2: What word?

MINISTER 3: "Froideur". She'd prefer – "coldness".

MINISTER 2: She's not very cosmopolitan, is she?

MINISTER 3: Oh no. Very provincial.

> **MINISTERS** *exit. Sfx: car on drive.* **ELSPETH** *and* **GEOFFREY** *enter.* **ELSPETH** *looks out window.* **GEOFFREY** *wears a chunky knitted sweater with a picture of Chevening, in rolling hills, embroidered on the front.*

ELSPETH: Oh God it's Alan Clark.

GEOFFREY: I do apologise. He insisted.

> **ELSPETH** *exits. Fx: dog barks.*

ALAN: *(Offstage.)* Get off me you little shit!

ELSPETH: *(Offstage.)* Summit! Summit! Down boy!

> **ALAN** *enters, followed by* **ELSPETH**.

ALAN: *(Brushing leg.)* God almighty.

GEOFFREY: Hello Alan. Sorry about that.

ALAN: Now I know how you feel after a session with Margaret.

ELSPETH: Drink Alan? Dinner at six Geoffrey. Sprouts and lamb.

ALAN: That's in ten minutes.

ELSPETH: I know. Drink?

ALAN: *(Eyeing her up.)* I fancy a nice…tasty, mature, white. You?

ELSPETH: Rancid old plonk? No thanks.

ALAN: Ha!

> **ELSPETH** *exits.*

ALAN: Good to see you Geoffrey. Even if it's not mutual. Ooh! Nice pullover. What is it?

GEOFFREY: This place. I had it commissioned. From a woman who knits.

ALAN: Sweet! You love it here don't you?

GEOFFREY: As does Elspeth.

ALAN: Look I come in peace. Seen the papers?

GEOFFREY: Yes.

ALAN: And?

GEOFFREY: They've been predicting my imminent demise for weeks.

ALAN: What are you going to do?

GEOFFREY: What business is it of yours?

ALAN: I have – thoughts. Useful ones. For the good of the party.

GEOFFREY: Go on.

ALAN: You've got to hang in there. It's essential. You're the only one with enough support in the party to block Michael bloody Heseltine if something happens. It'd be a disaster if she goes and the bastard might just swing it from what I'm hearing. You've got to hold on, stand firm alongside her. You know, benign synthesis.

GEOFFREY: I beg your pardon?

> **ELSPETH**, *who has returned, hands* **ALAN** *his drink.*

ALAN: Thanks darling. Hegel's Theory of Tension. Benign synthesis is the result of the co-existing presence of thesis and antithesis. She's the thesis, you're the antithesis, end result, benign synthesis.

GEOFFREY: Well I can assure you I will be "hanging on in there" as you put it.

ALAN: Good. Coz we don't want that wild eyed Zombie fucking things up. *(Beat.)* Michael bloody Heseltine. The man who buys his own furniture. Ha!

GEOFFREY: Why do you hate him?

ALAN: He strangles dogs for God's sake. Put it this way: she hates him, therefore, so do I.

GEOFFREY: Well you need worry no further. *(Beat.)* About my departure.

ALAN: Why?

GEOFFREY: Worry no more.

ALAN: Come on Geoffrey this is important. I've heard things too you know. You tell me, I tell you.

GEOFFREY: I have had assurances.

ALAN: From who?

GEOFFREY: May I politely refer you to my earlier answer?

ALAN: I'm only trying to help.

GEOFFREY: If you say so.

ALAN: Can I say something else?

GEOFFREY: Hmm?

ALAN: You could turn it down on Europe a bit.

GEOFFREY: *(Beat.)* Anything else?

ALAN: It's just a bit misguided. Out of step.

GEOFFREY: With whom?

ALAN: The man on the Clapham Omnibus. He doesn't give a shit about Europe. We do live on an island you know.

GEOFFREY: I'm not sure a man who went to Eton and lives in a castle is best placed to take the pulse of the British people.

ALAN: Neither is a jumped up little Welshman who lives in a place like this.

GEOFFREY: I owe my surroundings to merit Alan, unlike you, but we digress. I shall not be "easing up" on Europe because that is where our future lies.

ALAN: God you're boring! And wrong! Any system that pays French Farmers tons of money to sit on their fat arses all day is a bit flawed if you ask me.

GEOFFREY: You're not very good on detail are you? Have you actually read the Common Agricultural Policy?

ALAN: Oh fuck off Geoffers. I've got better things to do.

GEOFFREY: Alan if you and your allies persist with this bile it could seriously affect our party's future. If Labour can split in two, it's not entirely fanciful that the same fate could befall us.

ALAN: What, some kind of breakaway party for Euro-sceptics? That's never gonna happen.

GEOFFREY: Is that stupid *and* boring? Or has stupid replaced boring?

ALAN: No they're coexisting. Along with smug.

GEOFFREY: Let me put it in a way even you can understand. There is a party going on with much wine, women and song, and we have been invited. And we have accepted. Indeed we have arrived and are in the hallway. But we are now haggling over the terms of the invite. And the people who invited us are, understandably, getting a little impatient, because we are not behaving reasonably. How's that?

ALAN: Why should we care what a bunch of fucking foreigners think?

GEOFFREY: Thank you for reminding me of the challenge we face. To erase the word 'foreigner', indeed 'fucking foreigner' from our language. The same 'foreigner' whose wine and cheese you so avidly eat and drink. Talking of which. *(To* **ELSPETH***.)* How are the 'Brussels'?

ALAN: Oh ha ha.

ELSPETH: *(Beat.)* Well done. Very well done.

ALAN: If only you were more like this in public Geoffers.

GEOFFREY: You don't *have* to paddle in the shallow end of the pool you know.

    GEOFFREY *exits.*

ALAN: *(Calling after him.)* Least I'll never be out of my depth. *(To* **ELSPETH***.)* Not very feminist is it? Doing the cooking.

ELSPETH: I don't think you've quite got the hang of feminism.

ALAN: Really? All right then. If you're such a feminist, why d'you hate her?

ELSPETH: Who?

ALAN: Margaret.

ELSPETH: I don't.

ALAN: Yes you bloody do. You're like two wasps in a jam jar.

ELSPETH: I don't hate her Alan.

ALAN: Okay why'd you disapprove of her?

ELSPETH: I don't. Rather patronising isn't it? To 'disapprove' of a Prime Minister?

ALAN: What word would you use then?

ELSPETH: *(Beat.)*You could say I'm disappointed.

ALAN: Even more patronising. Ha! I knew it was a feminist thing.

ELSPETH: And what is a "feminist thing"?

ALAN: People like you putting out the idea that women should be the equal of men but when a woman not only equals a man but surpasses him, slagging her off because deep down you're just jealous thereby proving why feminism's a load of shit to start with because it's based on the idea that men and women are the same when clearly they're not, because women have tits and are jealous of women like Margaret whereas men have cocks and admire women like Margaret.

ELSPETH: I don't agree entirely. I'm not sure all those coal miners with cocks admire her.

ALAN: I'm talking generally.

ELSPETH: And remind me how many women there are in her cabinet again? Out of, what is it, eighteen? Nought is it? Or one?

ALAN: That's coz none of them are good enough my love.

ELSPETH: I agree on that. What intelligent woman *is* good at adultery, lying and saying 'yes' all the time?

ALAN: Feisty! Bottom line though, only dogs are feminists coz they can't get a man to fancy them so they take up feminism instead coz it gives 'em something to do. Present company excepted.

ELSPETH: I'm so flattered. What a tragedy you can't stay for dinner.

ALAN: I know. In fact *(Looks her up and down.)* d'you know, if you weren't with Geoffrey I'd –

ELSPETH: Please Alan. I wouldn't want to catch anything. And I don't sleep with the B team.

ALAN: Meeow! I'm enjoying this. Really enjoying this.

ELSPETH: You're a pervert aren't you?

ALAN: Darling our party's full of pervs. But I'm not one of 'em. I like 'em female for a start. And legal. *(Eyes her up again.)* Have you a got a sister?

ELSPETH: Have you got a wife?

ALAN: What's that got to do with it?

ELSPETH: She's probably expecting you.

ALAN: You're hot. Piping! Stick in there Geoffers. Enjoyed that.

GEOFFREY: Thank you Alan. I shall. And I didn't.

ALAN peers at the top of GEOFFREY's head.

ALAN: Is that Elspeth's thumbprint on your head? I'll see myself out. Toodle pip! *(Exits.)*

ELSPETH: Have you received assurances?

GEOFFREY: Indeed.

ELSPETH: From whom?

GEOFFREY: The Chief Whip.

ELSPETH: And you believe him?

GEOFFREY: Yes. He said the 1922 Committee told her not to change any of us – any of the top three, that is.

ELSPETH: Yes but Chief Whips come with horns and a tail don't they? Shouldn't you be expecting the unexpected?

GEOFFREY: If you expect the unexpected it is no longer unexpected.

ELSPETH: Stop being a lawyer Geoffrey. This is Margaret remember. Think Caligula.

GEOFFREY: And you of course are Lady Macbeth. According to the papers.

ELSPETH: I know. I just think you overestimate her loyalty that's all.

GEOFFREY: If you say so.

ELSPETH: I'm just saying, you know how it works. You of all people.

GEOFFREY: Thank you. Dinner?

They exit.

SCENE 10

Days later. **STEPHEN** *enters.*

STEPHEN: Something came up. Was it good news? Was it bad? We weren't really sure.

GEOFFREY *enters, humming.*

The Prime Minister wants to see you.

GEOFFREY: What about?

STEPHEN: Didn't say.

GEOFFREY: I'll go the back way.

STEPHEN *exits.* **GEOFFREY** *walks to* **MARGARET**'s, *who is in her office and readying herself. Sfx: knock at door.*

MARGARET: Come in!

GEOFFREY: Prime Minister.

MARGARET: Geoffrey do come in. Make yourself comfortable, may I get you anything?

GEOFFREY: I'm fine thank you Margaret.

MARGARET: Now Geoffrey I want to get straight to the point. I am making changes and I want you to be the first to know as they involve the Foreign Office. As you know we are bringing television cameras into the House and so the Leadership of the House will be terribly important and I want you to be in charge of it all. The alternative is the Home Office but I don't think you've expressed any interest in that? Have you? *(Beat.)* Geoffrey?

GEOFFREY: *(Trying to compose himself.)* I haven't. Really contemplated either. Is not the Foreign Office still the right place?

MARGARET: That option is no longer open.

GEOFFREY: Why?

MARGARET: We need change Geoffrey. A younger face. We are always looking to regenerate. We need to re-energise, refresh, from time to time.

GEOFFREY: Who did you have in mind? To replace me?

MARGARET: I'm afraid I can't say as I haven't told his boss yet. The relevant people do need to be informed first as you will appreciate.

GEOFFREY: Is this because of our meeting? Before Madrid? With Nigel?

MARGARET: It is *a* factor but there are many, although I did find your behaviour at that nasty little occasion alarming, not to say quite disloyal. I just do not have confidence that we can work together on the main issues any more. It is about trust Geoffrey. But this is not a demotion. The Leadership of the House is important and you will take charge of several cabinet committees. You will continue to have influence, power. *(Beat.)* What do you say?

GEOFFREY: *(Disoriented.)* I think I –

MARGARET: I shall need an answer soon Geoffrey.

GEOFFREY: I shall have to discuss it with Elsp – my team. I must say I – .

MARGARET: Geoffrey I quite understand, you need time. You must take as long as you like but I will need an answer in the next twenty-four hours. I want to get it sorted before it starts to leak. *(Beat.)* How is Elspeth by the way?

GEOFFREY: She is good.

MARGARET: Good. You have done a fine job as Foreign Secretary and we shall always be grateful. Our government, the party, this country, owe you a great deal.

GEOFFREY *starts to exit.*

MARGARET: Oh and Geoffrey?

GEOFFREY: Yes?

MARGARET: You will leave Chevening. It will have to be done quickly. But we'll find you somewhere else. Is that all right?

GEOFFREY *stunned, exits, walks back to office, stares into space.* **STEPHEN** *enters.*

STEPHEN: Are you all right?

GEOFFREY: Would you call Elspeth? And Ian Gow.

STEPHEN: Is that wise?

GEOFFREY: He is my oldest friend.

STEPHEN: And incredibly loyal to Margaret.

GEOFFREY: Yes but he is a good man. And wise. And it would do no harm to let her know our thinking.

STEPHEN: Of course.

Exits. **GEOFFREY** *contemplates.* **STEPHEN**, **ELSPETH** *and* **IAN** *enter.*

GEOFFREY: *(Takes deep breath.)* We have a dilemma. I have been offered the Leadership of the House but am minded not to take it. I – think, I am going to resign. But I would value your thoughts.

STEPHEN: What, resign from the government you mean? From the cabinet? From everything?

GEOFFREY: Yes. I shall sit on the backbenches and no longer be part of this government.

STEPHEN: Is that wise?

GEOFFREY: I don't see how I can carry on in Cabinet after this.

IAN: Geoffrey I am so desperately sorry. But look if you go to the back benches it'll be over. Oblivion. You're sixty-three. If you stay in cabinet you can alter the course of events. You'll have power. On the backbenches you'll be just another clapped-out footballer shouting unwanted advice from the terraces.

ELSPETH: He might have quite a lot of power. King across the water.

GEOFFREY: You are very much echoing what Margaret said, Ian.

IAN: I think she's right.

ELSPETH: You always do.

IAN: Not always. I am one of the few who gives it to her straight. But on this, I agree.

ELSPETH: But you only want to keep him in the cabinet for appearances. To give the illusion of unity.

IAN: I hesitate to use the word but I honestly believe at key moments like these the party and the government need and deserve Geoffrey's loyalty.

ELSPETH: Come on Ian loyalty's a two way thing. I mean, where's yours, now? *(Beat.)* I'm sorry that was unfair.

IAN: It's all right. It's all right Elspeth. I if were you, I'd be bloody fuming. But look he's got to stay. He's her protector, mad as it sounds. He makes her – palatable.

GEOFFREY: Stephen?

STEPHEN: I agree. If you resigned, it could be seen as churlish. She'd say you were ungrateful because you turned down a good job.

ELSPETH: But who wouldn't resign after the way he's been treated? I'd have thought he'd have everyone's sympathy.

STEPHEN: But it would be seen as disloyal by the people who matter.

ELSPETH: Disloyal? The Prime Minister has just sack–. Dispensed with the services of the man who rescued her, who stood by her since the beginning, but *he's* disloyal?

STEPHEN: Perception is seldom reality. But think about it. If he goes, the party will be much weaker. And if the foundations collapse, he'd never be forgiven. By supporters, let alone enemies.

ELSPETH: Whose foundations are we talking about? Hers or the Government's?

STEPHEN: Possibly both.

ELSPETH: If it were just hers that collapsed, would that be a price worth paying?

STEPHEN: Possibly. But remember: he who wields the dagger never wears the crown.

ELSPETH: Doesn't it depend who's wielding it?

IAN: *(Beat.)* You are in a position to bargain.

GEOFFREY: What do you mean?

IAN: Well, she wants you to stay. So use it and say okay, I want the Deputy Prime Minister-ship too. There is a vacancy.

ELSPETH: But it's a non-job isn't it? A title.

IAN: It is a constitutional fiction yes, but the job's what you make it. There is no reason why Deputy Prime Minister should not be, as the title suggests, the second most powerful person in the land. *(Beat.)* Do you know who's replacing you? As Foreign Secretary?

GEOFFREY: She wouldn't say. Said she hasn't told his boss yet.

STEPHEN: *(Beat.)* That'll be Major then.

ELSPETH: What!

IAN: John Major? Don't be ridiculous.

GEOFFREY: He's right you know. The Foreign Secretary has to come from inside the Cabinet. And the only member of the Cabinet with a boss is the Chief Secretary to the Treasury. John Major.

IAN: But that's absurd. Foreign Secretary? He doesn't even go abroad for his holidays. Jesus.

GEOFFREY: It is hard to believe. But we must not hold that against him. *(Beat.)* Stephen, we'll need to make arrangements.

STEPHEN: Of course.

GEOFFREY: Thank you Ian.

IAN: Geoffrey this shouldn't have happened. You're a fine man old chum. Look I know how you – *(Struggling.)* You know I do.

GEOFFREY: Thank you.

ELSPETH: Gentlemen would you give us some time?

    STEPHEN, **IAN** *exit.* **GEOFFREY** *sobs.*

ELSPETH: Are you all right?

GEOFFREY: I will be.

ELSPETH: I am so sorry.

GEOFFREY: This is the end.

ELSPETH: This is politics. And the Chief Whip is a liar.

GEOFFREY: I am surprised. I no longer consider him a friend.

ELSPETH: You are a great man and a great politician. And no one will blame you for walking away.

GEOFFREY: I worry what lies beyond the exit.

ELSPETH: It will be fine. What matters now is the manner of your leaving. And this will be a dignified departure, on your terms.

GEOFFREY: May I say how grateful I am for your constancy Elspeth? It means everything to me. I could not do without it. I know that duty and ambition mean I have not been the most attentive spouse. Or parent. I know that.

They embrace.

ELSPETH: I knew what to expect when we married. But that's not why my fingers were crossed.

GEOFFREY: Thank you.

ELSPETH: Let's go to Chevening tonight.

GEOFFREY: *(Beat.)* She wants us to move out. Immediately.

ELSPETH: *(Shocked.)* What? Why?

GEOFFREY: Spite, I suspect.

ELSPETH: My God. That rather seals it. Doesn't it?

ELSPETH *exits.*

GEOFFREY *left contemplating.*

Act 2

SCENE 1

Months later. **GEOFFREY** *and* **BRIAN WALDEN** *in a TV studio. Theme to "Weekend World" plays.*

WALDEN: Good afternoon. Welcome to Weekend World. My guest is the Deputy Pwime Minister. But, what exactly is his wole? How much twouble is he prepared to make? And how does he weally get on with Mrs Thatcher? Let's ask him. Sir Geoffwey Howe, what is your welationship with the Pwime Minister?

GEOFFREY: Fruitful. Ongoing. We have always had a productive relationship as history will show.

WALDEN: Even though she sacked you?

GEOFFREY: She did not. I was offered the jobs of Deputy Prime Minister and Leader of the House which, after consideration, I felt I could not turn down.

WALDEN: Yes but let me put this to you. It's a demotion isn't it? The title 'Deputy Pwime Minister' is just a bauble. A meaningless bauble.

GEOFFREY: I don't think you'll find many who would describe the Deputy Prime Ministership of the United Kingdom as a meaningless bauble.

WALDEN: But it is, some would say, a bit of a come down. One minute you're discussing Bwitain's wole in Euwope with the likes of Monsieur Delors, the next you're discussing *(Looks at notes.)* "Women's hairdwessing facilities and toilets in the Palace of Westminster."

GEOFFREY: Which is, if I may say, an important issue. It is unacceptable that female members of the House are not adequately catered for in matters of – *(Hesitates.)* that department.

WALDEN: Allwight, so you're Deputy Pwime Minister. Your pwoblem is this. It's a vewy impwessive *sounding* wole, but a wole with no weal power. That's twue, isn't it?

GEOFFREY: Not at all. I have a good deal of power. I am on a number of important cabinet committees, shaping the agenda for the decade to come.

WALDEN: But what's the point of being on those committees if she ignores them?

GEOFFREY: That's not how government works Mr Walden.

WALDEN: It's how this one works isn't it?

GEOFFREY: No it is not.

WALDEN: So you haven't been side-lined? You're not being ignored?

GEOFFREY: No I am not. *(Tetchy.)* I am kept fully up to date on all matters of importance.

WALDEN: Allwight then. Now. If you had to give one bit of advice to the Pwime Minister, what would it be? On her style of leadership, for example? Because that's your pwoblem, isn't it? She's divisive. We know she is. So what about that?

GEOFFREY: When you have a leader with the sense of purpose Margaret has, one is bound to divide opinion but if one heeds critics too much one risks staunching the healthy flow of ideas that makes Thatcherism successful. Indeed I like to say that all the trendy "isms" of the last decade are now "wasms", thanks to Thatcherism. *(Looks pleased.)* Even so, the Conservative case must be put carefully. We must win friends, as well as battles.

GEOFFREY uneasy: realises gaffe.

WALDEN: Aha! We'll be back after the bweak.

Music Sting.

WALDEN: Thank you Geoffrey. You all wight?

GEOFFREY: Fine. You getting what you want?

WALDEN: Oh yes. It's wonderful. Everyone knows you hate each other and you're desperately twying to pwetend you don't, so it makes gweat – theatre. If I may say.

GEOFFREY: *(Beat.)* I don't hate her.

PRODUCER'S VOICE: Coming to you in ten Brian.

WALDEN: What it is then? If not hate?

PRODUCER'S VOICE: Coming to you in five Brian.

GEOFFREY: I. *(Beat.)* Admire her. Greatly.

Weekend World Sting plays.

WALDEN: Welcome back.

Black out. **MINISTER 2** *enters.*

MINISTER 1: Poor old Geoffrey. Even when he tried to defend her he attacked her.

MINISTER 2: Yes. The papers were full of it. *(To audience.)* "Howe in coded attack on Thatcher's style of leadership." "Deputy warns PM on dangers of not listening." That kind of thing.

MINISTER 1: *(To audience.)* The union is in danger.

MINISTER 2: Indeed.

MINISTER 1: So where are we now?

MINISTER 2: Geoffrey's new residence. It's nice – but it's not Chevening.

SCENE 2

GEOFFREY *working. Bell. Barking.*

GEOFFREY: *(Calling.)* Ian's here.

ELSPETH: *(Off stage.)* Drinks? Large or small?

GEOFFREY: Large.

ELSPETH: *(Off stage, warmly.)* Ian!

IAN: *(Off stage.)* Elspeth! *(Beat.)* Summit you bloody psychopath!

ELSPETH *and* **IAN** *enter, arm in arm.*

GEOFFREY: Ian how lovely to see you.

IAN: Ditto old chum. *(Looking around as he sits down.)* Settling in?

47

GEOFFREY: Well enough. But I wouldn't pretend to you of all people that we don't miss the old place.

IAN: I did convey your feelings. *(Beat.)* I shall still love her all my days though. How's the job?

GEOFFREY: It has its compensations.

ELSPETH *enters with drinks tray.*

ELSPETH: Drambuies.

IAN: *(Looks round.)* Clearly! Thank you.

ELSPETH: So. Another peace mission.

IAN: *(Sighs.)* Do you know I feel like a horse with ropes pulling its front legs one way and its back legs another.

ELSPETH: You should be used to it by now.

IAN: Yes but it's never been quite so – ferocious. My two dearest friends in the world and I'm caught in the middle.

GEOFFREY: *(Glances at **ELSPETH**.)* Yes. A conflict of loyalty. Now you know how I feel.

IAN: I mean, if *my* blood and guts get spilt, who cares? But if the party's entrails gushed out? Ghastly. No political surgeon in the world could sew 'em back in.

GEOFFREY: Your substantive point is?

IAN: We're not in court old chum.

GEOFFREY: Sorry. You were saying.

IAN: You need to ease up.

ELSPETH: Shouldn't you be telling her that?

IAN: I am treating the patient I think most likely to respond.

GEOFFREY: And what medicine are you recommending?

IAN: I don't know. One that stops you signalling your differences in public. I mean, do you really need to *air* your grievances?

GEOFFREY: Yes. Subtly.

IAN: Why?

GEOFFREY: Because as you know, if it's done in private, one tends to be at best ignored or at worst insulted.

IAN: Yes but the battle's won isn't it? Over Europe. It's not like we're going to quit or anything.

GEOFFREY: True.

IAN: It would be too complicated for a start. Un-doing all those treaties. Like the political equivalent of reversing a vasectomy. Very messy.

GEOFFREY: That's rather good. I must use that on Alan Clark next time I see him.

They laugh.

ELSPETH: And when will that be?

GEOFFREY: Never hopefully. But I tell you what. There will be no *(Air quotes.)* "Euro-reversal" in my lifetime. Not if I can help it.

IAN: Euro-reversal? Wouldn't it be, "Eur-exit"?

ELSPETH: No! Too ugly sounding. Too many harsh syllables.

IAN: What would you call it then?

Silence/shrugging of shoulders.

ELSPETH: Couldn't we do the Hokey-Cokey on Europe?

GEOFFREY: What do you mean?

ELSPETH: You know. Half in, half out. *(Semi-sings: badly.)* "You put your right leg in, your right leg out –

IAN: In out, in out, shake it all about!

ELSPETH: You do the Hokey-Cokey and you turn around –

GEOFFREY/ELSPETH/IAN: – that's what it's all about!

Laughter.

49

GEOFFREY: No that would never work.

IAN: In that case what about the Shipping Forecast? Mild turbulence, decreasing slowly.

GEOFFREY: Ha ha ha. No.

IAN: She thinks you're being obstructive Geoffrey.

GEOFFREY: Obstructive?

IAN: Yes. In cabinet. Obstructive. That's the exact word she used. You don't speak much and when you do your contributions are generally negative.

GEOFFREY: I see.

IAN: All I'm saying is, there's no harm in being a bit less Eeyore and a bit more Tigger. *(Beat.)* Look I know it's going to end one day. I'm just trying to keep the show on the road for as long as I can. And for that to happen you and her need to be in it. You know that prayer we said at school? "May there never be wanting, a due supply of persons, to serve God, both in Church, and state"? You are very well qualified to serve God, Geoffrey. And so is she. Everything else is secondary. Isn't it?

ELSPETH: That's cheating Ian. Bringing God and your old school into it.

GEOFFREY: I can reassure you somewhat. I will continue to fight the good fight inside the ring as it were.

IAN: Thank you.

GEOFFREY: Even if it is a little one sided. Margaret has the world's most powerful newspaper proprietor on side. And Bernard. An unusually generous Yorkshire man who is feeding Mr. Murdoch's dogs of war all the red meat they can eat.

IAN: And you're a nice bit of steak.

GEOFFREY: Precisely.

IAN: You've got Elspeth.

GEOFFREY: Even she might be hard pressed to stop me getting burnt to a cinder.

IAN: What, like Joan of Arc?

GEOFFREY: If you say so.

ELSPETH: Thomas More perhaps.

GEOFFREY: But one does yearn for recognition, not recrimination.

IAN: Well we've got to keep you off Murdoch's barbie that's for sure.

ELSPETH: Geoffrey, could you get some more ice?

She hands him glass. He exits.

(Urgently.) You've got to do something. Did you hear about Balmoral? The Queen?

IAN: *(Hedging bets.)* I might have.

ELSPETH: They made that announcement about joining the ERM without even telling him. He only found out when the Queen asked what he thought. He had to pretend. Can you imagine? Bluffing in front of Her Majesty? She knew exactly what was happening. Most embarrassing.

IAN: I can imagine.

GEOFFREY enters, IAN splutters.

I can imagine – it must be hard getting used to this place.

GEOFFREY: So. Balmoral.

IAN smiles: looks at ELSPETH. She rolls her eyes.

IAN: Yes. Unfortunate.

GEOFFREY: It is disconcerting, to say the least, to find out things of such importance, via *(Beat.)* "A Third Party".

IAN: Bet Her Majesty's never been called that before.

ELSPETH: He's not being unreasonable is he?

IAN: Unreasonable? *(Beat.)* Have I told you about the Great Tuck Shop Scandal? *(ELSPETH looks blank.)* Right. Both new boys trying to fit in, and Geoffrey's accused of something quite appalling. Fraud, wasn't it?

GEOFFREY: Effectively yes.

IAN: He was innocent of course, and whereas most of us would be screaming and crying, he was Gandhi. First he turns out his pockets. Then goes through the sums, penny by penny, gobstopper by gobstopper, 'till he's proved to the Dragon in charge that he's right and she's wrong. Wonderful.

GEOFFREY: Sadly, my dragon-persuading skills are not what they were.

IAN: How old were you Geoff? Thirteen?

GEOFFREY: Thirteen and a half.

IAN: Brilliant.

ELSPETH: He could have left months ago you know. He should have left months ago.

IAN: I can see why you think that.

ELSPETH: Does *she* though? Does she care what people think?

IAN: Yes actually. Real people. Publicans and housewives and builders. We care too of course. But we don't *understand* them like her. Because let's be honest, we're not like them, are we? *(Beat.)* It's the enemy she doesn't care about. But then did Winston lie awake at night worrying about Germans? I mean what would this country would be like if not for her? We'd be bloody ploughing fields and speaking Russian by now. She saved us. Geoffrey too, but she *(Beat.)* led us.

ELSPETH: *(Beat.)* Is she in trouble?

IAN: She needs to be careful. And I've told her so. But it's the dashers she listens to: you know, Clarky. Parky.

GEOFFREY: If only Monsieur Delors could dash.

IAN: Oh she can't stand that man.

GEOFFREY: Needs him though. She needs enemies to thrive.

ELSPETH: What happens when she runs out of enemies?

IAN: What happens when she runs out of friends.

ELSPETH: She's lucky to have you Ian. So are we.

IAN: *(Shaking hands.)* Good to see you old chum. Fight the good fight.

ELSPETH: *(Embracing **IAN**.)* Goodbye Ian.

They gaze fondly in the direction of his exit. Huge explosion.

BBC RADIO VOICE: The Conservative politician Ian Gow has been killed by a car bomb at his home in East Sussex. The IRA have claimed responsibility. *(Fade.)* The device went off…

*The phone rings. **GEOFFREY** answers.*

GEOFFREY: Yes. *(Beats.)* Yes. *(Beats.)* Yes I see.

(Beats.) Thank you. *(Hangs up.)*

GEOFFREY *and* **ELSPETH** *hold eachother.* **MARGARET** *enters.*

GEOFFREY: I'm sorry Margaret.

MARGARET: He was such a good man Geoffrey. To have him taken like this. By such evil.

ELSPETH: He loved you Margaret. Really loved you. He had so much life, so much force. I can't imagine the world without him.

All three lost in their own thoughts/ grief.

SCENE 3

MINISTERS 1 *and* **2** *create the commons for PMQs.*

MINISTER 1: The glue that bound them together, just, was gone.

MINISTER 2: I know. And just when you thought things couldn't get any worse.

GEOFFREY *and* **MARGARET** *enter.* **ELSPETH** *wrapped against the cold, with placard: "no to homelessness".*

SPEAKER'S VOICE: Order! Order! Questions to the Prime Minister. Question number one.

MARGARET *stands, imperious. A* **HACK** *enters.*

HACK: Colin from The Sun. Mrs Howe can I just ask a few fings? 'Bout your campaign.

ELSPETH: Yes of course. But it's not my campaign, it's St Mungo's.

HACK: Yeah, sure, sure.

MARGARET: Mr Speaker sir. This morning I had meetings with Ministerial colleagues and others. In addition to my duties in this House I shall be having further meetings later today.

SPEAKER'S VOICE: Order! Mr John Redwood!

REDWOOD'S VOICE: Does my right honourable friend really believe European Monetary Union will happen and if so would it be good for Britain?

MARGARET: Mr Speaker anyone who believes the British Parliament will agree to a single currency is quite frankly on the way to cloud cuckoo land.

Uproar: shouts of "hear hear!" **GEOFFREY** *fidgets uncomfortably.*

HACK: Wossit for? What's the point I mean?

ELSPETH: The point is, every night in London up to a thousand people sleep rough and that is terrible, so we've decided to sleep on the streets ourselves for a week to draw attention to their plight.

SPEAKER'S VOICE: Order! Order! Mr Neil Kinnock! *(Cheers/boos.)*

KINNOCK'S VOICE: Mr Speaker, will the Prime Minister condemn those Conservative MPs who have publically insulted her Deputy simply for expressing his views on the European Community? *(Cheers/boos.)*

SPEAKER'S VOICE: Order!

MARGARET: Mr Speaker, unlike the right honourable gentleman's party, we value the great British tradition of free speech very much indeed. We have not, and never will, punish our members simply for expressing their views. *(Cheers/boos.)* Unlike the party opposite!

SPEAKER'S VOICE: Order! Kinnock!

KINNOCK'S VOICE: Mr Speaker let me try again. Does she not owe it to her Deputy Prime Minister to say he enjoys her full confidence?

MARGARET: Mr Speaker The Deputy Prime Minister is too big a man to need a little man like the Right Honourable Gentleman to stand up for him. *(Cheers/boos.)*

GEOFFREY *hardens: she is clearly not backing him.*

KINNOCK'S VOICE: Thank you Mr Speaker I think that says it all!

HACK: Bit ironic isn't it, that it's your husband's policies that caused the homelessness in their first place?

ELSPETH: No, because my husband's policies didn't.

HACK: Lot of people say they did.

ELSPETH: And this person, says they didn't.

SPEAKER'S VOICE: Order!

REDWOOD-TYPE VOICE: Mr Speaker after her triumph at the Rome Summit does my right honourable friend agree with me that our pound sterling is a cause worth fighting for?

More cheers and boos: **GEOFFREY** *even more uncomfortable.*

MARGARET: Mr Speaker it would be totally and utterly wrong to abolish the pound sterling. *(More cheers than boos.)* It is the greatest expression of sovereignty we have. *(Cheers.)*

MINISTER 1'S VOICE: Look at Geoffrey!

MINISTER 2'S VOICE: He's squirming!

MARGARET: We have surrendered quite enough. *(Cheers.)* We will not let Monsieur Delors and the European Commission extinguish our democracy. We will simply not give in.

Uproar: **GEOFFREY** *gets up, wanders over to* **ELSPETH**.

HACK: Whose did then? I mean, whose policies did cause homelessness? Thatcher's?

ELSPETH: I'm not going to fall for that. I'm a campaigner not a
politician.

HACK: All right then. Are you not bovvered your "campaigning" is gonna
embarrass your 'u'sband?

ELSPETH: No, far from it. My husband is proud of me. And I am proud
of him.

> **GEOFFREY** *looks back:* **MARGARET** *standing up. Cheers, boos.*

MARGARET: Mr. Delors said he wanted the European Parliament to be
the democratic body of the Community, he wanted the Commission
to be the Executive and he wanted the Council of Ministers to be the
Senate. No! No! No!

> **GEOFFREY** *looks at* **ELSPETH**, *then* **MARGARET**. *He has had enough.*
> **GEOFFREY**, **ELSPETH**, **HACK/ MINISTERS** *exit.* **MARGARET** *at*
> *her desk.*

SCENE 4

GEOFFREY *enters.*

MARGARET: Geoffrey do sit down.

GEOFFREY: I think you know why I am here Margaret.

MARGARET: Is there anything we could do to change your mind?

GEOFFREY: I am afraid not.

MARGARET: I am aware of our differences Geoffrey but you must not
take the theatre of the Commons too seriously. It need not lead to
this. A strong government needs a variety of views and we can ill
afford to lose a man of your calibre.

GEOFFREY: That is very kind of you Margaret.

MARGARET: I mean it. I would be happy for you to reconsider.

GEOFFREY: That is very decent of you but there is no turning back, you
might say.

MARGARET: Geoffrey you do realise you are out of touch on this? If you asked the people, they would say our future lies outside Europe if anything. Or on the edges.

GEOFFREY: The people are not always right Margaret as you know.

MARGARET: You know what Winston said don't you?

GEOFFREY: Remind me?

MARGARET: "We are with Europe, but not of it. Linked but not combined. Interested and associated, but not absorbed."

GEOFFREY: Winston was a great leader. A great wartime leader. But this is not a war.

MARGARET: Oh but it is Geoffrey. It's just that there are no guns. *(Beat.)* Very well. Would you like a drink?

GEOFFREY: Thank you but I will need all my wits about me for what is to follow, I suspect.

MARGARET: Yes of course. *(Beat.)* Geoffrey you have been an outstanding member of this Government and I truly believe we might not be sitting here today were it not *for you*. You have achieved so much and your budget of 1981 will go down as one of the truly great budgets. It helped us get back on our feet again.

GEOFFREY: Thank you. It has been an honour and a privilege to serve alongside you. And I am proud of much of what we achieved, in Hong Kong, Gibraltar and the like.

MARGARET: Sixteen years, Geoffrey. It is sixteen years since I asked you to serve in the Shadow Cabinet. And our partnership has remained strong throughout. Until now.

GEOFFREY: Indeed Margaret.

MARGARET: A little like a marriage don't you think?

GEOFFREY: A little like some marriages perhaps.

Subtlety lost on **MARGARET**: *she looks blank, then turns harder.*

MARGARET: And how is your wife?

GEOFFREY: She is – fine.

MARGARET: Is she fine?

GEOFFREY: Yes.

MARGARET: Do thank her for me. For all she has done.

GEOFFREY: *(Beat.)* How best to inform the press?

MARGARET: I have spoken to Bernard. A joint release of letters at seven o'clock. Will that suit?

GEOFFREY: That will be fine, thank you.

They stand.

MARGARET: I am sorry it has come to this Geoffrey. But thank you.

GEOFFREY: Thank you Prime Minister.

They shake hands. She watches him go, sits. Lights dim, come back: she's still working.
INGHAM enters with file.

INGHAM: Morning Prime Minister.

MARGARET: Good morning Bernard.

INGHAM: How are you?

MARGARET: I am very good.

INGHAM: Good. No reason not to be. *(Consults file.)* Nothing to worry about. FT's worst, where is it now oh yes "the Thatcher edifice is in danger of falling apart" which might be worrying if anyone read the bloody thing, usual drivel in the Daily Mirror, few tributes to him, "tenacious, patient" that kind of thing, then the Times – this is more like it – "Mrs Thatcher's leadership remains robust, undaunted, unchallenged. Howe has been openly undermining her too long." And Hugo Young, this is good, where are we, oh yes, "sudden departures have become such a hallmark of the Thatcher years that Howe's is no longer one capable of shaking the Thatcher world". So. Business as usual.

MARGARET: Thank you Bernard. I am really rather disappointed Geoffrey has gone. And surprised. I wanted him to stay. But he thinks he is more important than he actually is and he is so very pompous. *(Beat.)* It is the treachery I find hardest to understand. The disloyalty. Now do the papers talk about that?

INGHAM: No. But they will tomorrow.

MARGARET: Good.

INGHAM: Not quite the end of it mind you. He's claiming he's lost his voice and he's not saying anything publically till Parliament's back next week. Says he owes it to the House to let them know reasons for his resignation first. So it'll rumble on a bit but we're not exactly quaking in our boots.

MARGARET: No. *(Quizzical.)* What was it Denis Healey said? About Geoffrey?

INGHAM: "Being attacked by Geoffrey Howe is like being savaged by a dead sheep."

MARGARET: Oh yes. *(Beat.)* Goodness me his wife is dreadful. NOT one of us.

INGHAM: She might be one o' them though. I think she's a bloody Communist meself. Lady Haw-Haw!

MARGARET: Very good Bernard.

INGHAM: Thank you Prime Minister. Anyway. Nothing to fear from a Geoffrey speech as I say. Apart from falling asleep. I mean, have you seen the Geoffrey Howe book of memorable quotes?

MARGARET: No?

INGHAM: Neither have I. Boom boom!

MARGARET *doesn't get it.*

As I say, nowt to worry about. "Dead Sheep with non-job, walks plank." Not exactly a crisis.

MARGARET: I agree Bernard. Thank you.

They exit.

SCENE 5

The **HOWES'** *home.* **GEOFFREY** *enters clutching a speech: he is rehearsing in his head, gesticulating. The TV is on.*

MARGARET: *(Sound from TV.)* "… Like a stubborn batsman I am still at the crease even though the bowling has been pretty hostile of late. And in case anyone doubted it I can assure you there will be no ducking the bouncers, no stonewalling, no playing for time. The bowling's going to get hit all round the ground. That's my style… " *(Applause.)*

ELSPETH *enters.*

ELSPETH: How's it looking?

GEOFFREY: Less than inspiring.

ELSPETH: People will respect you, you know. For not upsetting the apple cart.

GEOFFREY: Thank you.

ELSPETH: Do you regret it? Quitting I mean?

GEOFFREY: *(Beat.)* No. But the consequences become ever more apparent.

ELSPETH: What, loss of power?

GEOFFREY: I lost that when I left the Foreign Office. No, I was shown the ropes the other day. In the Commons. As a new backbencher. Where to sit, how to bag a place and so on. Like going back to school as a new boy after years as a prefect. Trifle humiliating.

ELSPETH: How can you be humiliated when you made the decision yourself?

GEOFFREY: The process – tends towards humiliation. Made me realise how unimportant I am. Now.

ELSPETH: But you're not.

GEOFFREY: Thank you. But it does rather feel like it. And going out with this *(Rustles speech.)* damp squib won't help. In front of one man and his dog.

ELSPETH: The chamber will be packed won't it?

GEOFFREY: Now I'm a back bencher I must wait my turn. And tomorrow it's the Queen's Speech Debate, which goes on 'til five o clock. By which time it will be me, Mr Speaker and a few diehards.

ELSPETH: And the cameras. So add a few million.

GEOFFREY: I doubt it. But convention forbids interruption, or heckling. So that at least is in my favour. Unlike this. *(Rustles speech.)* I am not, as we know, the most electrifying performer. Olivier rests easy in his grave.

ELSPETH: But you have passion. You're Welsh for goodness sake. Just because you keep it under control doesn't mean it's not there. Why d'you think I married you?

GEOFFREY: I sometimes ask myself that.

ELSPETH: Don't be silly.

GEOFFREY: I can't do fire and brimstone. I can't dazzle like –

They sit silent for a few seconds

ELSPETH: Yes but it's easier to dazzle when you're arguing *against* something Geoffrey. But you have something even more powerful. You believe in something. You really believe.

GEOFFREY: I feel constrained by loyalty. Michael Grylls sent me a note today. *(Gets note out.)* "Don't damage the PM, you'll only damage yourself and the country." I'm expected to pull my punches.

ELSPETH: Do you want to?

GEOFFREY: You know what will happen if I am honest.

ELSPETH: What?

GEOFFREY: It will destroy her.

ELSPETH: And?

GEOFFREY: I'm not sure I'm ready to do that.

ELSPETH: But you *are* ready to betray your own principles?

GEOFFREY: All my achievements will be forgotten. The budgets, Gibraltar, Hong Kong. I will be remembered… as Brutus.

ELSPETH: Not by everyone.

GEOFFREY: And there will be repercussions. Friends will turn against me. Against us. Because they love her more than they like me.

ELSPETH: There's no such thing as a friend in politics is there?

GEOFFREY: Perhaps. But in this conflict of loyalty, I fear that loyalty to leader and party trumps all. Arguably.

ELSPETH: *(Firm now.)* For God's sake Geoffrey what about loyalty to a cause? Your cause? It is a conflict, I can see that, but it's one you've, I don't know, wrestled with for too long. You've honoured your side of the bargain. You've done so much for her. And the party. And now when the thing you value most could be ruined you're not screwing your courage to the sticking place, you're letting it fail you. And tomorrow you have a chance, probably your only chance and certainly your best one, to do something about it. And because of a sense of duty, a misplaced sense of duty, you're not going to.

GEOFFREY: *(Beat.)* What you are saying then, is that I should be more of a wolf.

ELSPETH: Quite.

GEOFFREY: Albeit one in sheep's clothing.

ELSPETH: Ha! Very good. Yes, I suppose that is what I'm saying.

GEOFFREY: My old tutor wrote to me today.

ELSPETH: Oh yes?

GEOFFREY: He said there's no point in a civilised resignation which is soon forgotten. Make it count, he said. Make your resignation really, really count. If I do say what needs to be said – *if* – I will never twirl the Field Marshal's baton, of course.

ELSPETH: What would you think about that?

GEOFFREY: Sanguine. I think.

    GEOFFREY *contmplates his speech.*

SCENE 6

MINISTERS 1 and **2** enter.

MINISTER 1: Do you think he's going to stick the knife in?

MINISTER 2: No. Hasn't got the balls. Unlike you know who.

MINISTER 1: He will tow the line won't he? As in, *(Mimes quote marks.)* "this is a disagreement over presentation *not* policy". *(To audience.)* You know, style, not substance.

MINISTER 2: I hope so. I think so.

MINISTER 1: You know they brought his speech forward?

MINISTER 2: Really?

MINISTER 1: Yes. He's gone from bottom of the bill, to top. Opening the show! Someone in the Speaker's office changed the running order. At the last minute!

MINISTER 2: Procedural thing apparently.

MINISTER 1: Or a not-a-friend-of-Margaret thing.

MARGARET enters, sits down, for PMQs.

MINISTER 2: *(Checks watch. To audience.)* Oh just quickly, on the timing, bit worrying actually, nominations for the leadership of our party, you know, challengers to Margaret, have to be in by noon on Thursday –

MINISTER 1: *(Interrupts.)* the day after tomorrow.

MINISTER 2: – exactly, and it can only happen once a year if it happens at all and this year as I say the deadline is –

MINISTER 1: In 45 hours, 58 minutes.

MINISTER 2: Exactly. So if he did want to – *(Mimes knifing.)* now would be the perfect time.

MINISTER 1: Yes. Heseltine would be out of the traps like a greyhound.

MINISTER 2: Quite.

MINISTER 1: We need to– *(Points to seats. They sit.)*

SPEAKER'S VOICE: Order Order! Geoffrey Howe. I remind the House that a resignation statement is heard in silence, without interruption.

GEOFFREY puts on glasses.

GEOFFREY: Mr Speaker thank you. It has been suggested that I decided to resign solely because of questions of style and not on matters of substance at all. Indeed if some of my former colleagues are to be believed I must be the first Minister in history who has resigned because he was in full agreement with government policy.

Huge laugh. **MARGARET** *forces smile.*

GEOFFREY: Mr Speaker, the Prime Minister and I have shared together something like 700 meetings of cabinet or shadow cabinet over the last eighteen years, some 400 hours alongside each other and more than thirty international summit meetings. For both of us I suspect that's a pretty daunting record. The House might well feel that something more than simple matters of style would be necessary to rupture such a well tried relationship.

Let me first make clear an important point. I do not regard it as wrong for Britain to criticise matters of European policy in a style that is plain but courteous. Nor in any sense is it wrong for us to do alone. But it is here I fear, that my Right Honourable Friend the Prime Minister increasingly risks leading herself and others astray, in matters of substance as well as style.

Silence.

GEOFFREY: I have to say Mr Speaker I find rather troubling the nightmare image conjured up by my Right Honourable Friend, who seems sometimes to look out on a continent positively teeming with ill-intentioned people, scheming, in her words, to "extinguish democracy" or to "dissolve our national identities".

Intakes of breath, gasps.

GEOFFREY: What kind of vision is that Mr Speaker for our business people who trade there each day, for our financiers who seek to make London the money capital of Europe, or for all the young people of today? How on earth are the Chancellor of the Exchequer and the Governor of the Bank of England supposed to conduct complex negotiations in good faith with that kind of background noise? *(Murmurs.)* Mr Speaker I believe the Chancellor and the Governor are cricketing enthusiast so I hope there is no monopoly of cricketing metaphors. It is rather like sending your opening batsmen to the crease only for them to find, the moment the first balls are bowled, that their bats have been broken before the game by the team captain.

Laughter, gasps.

GEOFFREY: Mr Speaker, Cabinet Government is all about trying to persuade one another from within. I have tried to do that, as Foreign Secretary and since. But I now realise the task has become futile: of trying to stretch the meaning of words beyond what was credible, trying to pretend there was a common policy when every step forward risked being subverted by some casual comment or impulsive answer.

Murmurs: "unbelievable!" "Incredible!"

SPEAKER'S VOICE: Order! Order!

GEOFFREY *walks to the front of stage. This is his moment. He has grown in confidence, stature and self belief.*

GEOFFREY: My honourable friends, the conflict of loyalty, of loyalty to my Right Honourable Friend the Prime Minister – and in two decades together that instinct is still very real – and a loyalty to what I perceive to be the true interests of this nation, that conflict of loyalty has become all too great. I no longer believe it is possible to resolve that conflict from within this Government. That is why I resigned. In doing so, I have done what I believe to be right for my party and my country. The time has come for others to consider their own response to the tragic conflict of loyalties with which I have myself wrestled for perhaps too long.

Silence. **MARGARET** *stands, looks around her, gives* **GEOFFREY** *the death stare, exits.* **ALAN CLARK** *enters.*

ALAN: You shit. You pompous, back stabbing little shit. D'you know what makes it even more pathetic?

GEOFFREY: I think you're going to tell me.

ALAN: Her voice in every line. She fucking dictated it, didn't she.

GEOFFREY: Elspeth is not a dictator, Alan. Margaret, on the other hand …

ALAN: Wanker.

GEOFFREY: You of course have never slavishly done the bidding of a strong female leader.

ALAN: History will judge you very poorly for this.

GEOFFREY: That rather depends on who writes it. I think I'll come out of it rather well.

ALAN: Regicide. That's what it is. You've killed the Queen. Like some snivelling home counties Macbeth.

GEOFFREY: Except I'm Welsh.

ALAN: Even worse.

Exits. **ELSPETH** *enters.*

ELSPETH: Are you all right?

GEOFFREY: Yes. More than all right actually.

MINISTERS *enter.*

MINISTER 1: And so the deed was done.

MINISTER 2: Nine days later Margaret resigned.

MINISTER 1: And John Major became our Prime Minister.

MINISTER 3: Our next & final stop.

MINISTER 1: The other place.

MINISTER 2: The House of Lords.

Years later. **MARGARET** *enters.*

MARGARET: *(To* **ELSPETH**.*)* Hello dear. You don't mind me calling you 'dear' do you?

ELSPETH: Hello Lady Thatcher. No. Not at all.

MARGARET: Geoffrey! How nice to see you. Really. How long has it been?

GEOFFREY: I'm not sure. Years?

MARGARET: Now. What are we going to do about Europe for goodness' sake? All this talk about 'ever closer union'. Absolute rubbish!

GEOFFREY: Well – *(Beat.)* it's good to see you Margaret.

MARGARET: And what about Sarajevo? I am going to ask NATO to stop the Serbs. It is absolutely appalling. They are behaving like the Nazis. And I want you, I want you to do the same.

GEOFFREY: If you say so.

MARGARET: Geoffrey I do wish you would stop saying that.

GEOFFREY: What?

MARGARET: "If you say so." I must say I found it terribly irritating.

GEOFFREY: If you – sorry. The competition must have been rather stiff.

MARGARET: What do you mean?

GEOFFREY: Me saying – that, must have been very irritating. To have trumped everything else.

MARGARET: Oh I see. Yes. Do you know Geoffrey, I never thought you had it in you.

GEOFFREY: Neither did I, Margaret. Neither did I.

MARGARET exits. **GEOFFREY** *and* **ELSPETH** *embrace.*

She exits. **GEOFFREY** *reflects. Music. Birds sing.*

END

Salamander Street

Also available from Jonathan Maitland

The Last Temptation of Boris Johnson
Paperback 9781913630768
eBook 9781913630751

It was the dinner that changed history: the night in February 2016 when Boris Johnson decided to vote 'leave' and a nation's future was sealed. Guests included the spirits of Prime Ministers past including Margaret Thatcher, Winston Churchill and Tony Blair as well as fellow MP Michael Gove, the journalist Sarah Vine, Marina Wheeler and Evgeny Lebedev.

Fast forward to post-Brexit Britain, 2029. For reasons that may be fact and/or fiction at the time of the performance, Boris, no longer in power, roams the political wilderness. Unexpected events see him back in the spotlight and with a chance to "make Britain great again". This play addresses the big questions: What will Britain look like in ten years' time? Is chlorinated chicken really bad for you? Who does the NHS belong to and what IS going on inside the head of the most divisive and controversial politician of our time?

www.salamanderstreet.com